Published by Crown Publishers, Inc., 201 East 50th Street, New York, New York 10022.

Visit the Random House Web site at www.randomhouse.com

CROWN is a trademark of Crown Publishers, Inc.

The Civil War: Unstilled Voices is produced by becker&mayer!, Kirkland, Washington.

www.beckermayer.com

Edited by Jennifer Worick

Designed by Devorah Wolf • Art direction by Simon Sung

Production management by Kate Berger • Production by Victor Mingovits

Photo research by Jennifer Doyle • Additional artwork by Matt Hutnak

Printed and assembled in China.

Library of Congress Cataloging-in-Publication Data

Lawliss, Chuck.

    The Civil War : unstilled voices / by Chuck Lawliss. — 1st ed.

       p. cm.

    ISBN 0-609-60255-1

    1. United States—History—Civil War, 1861-1865 Miscellanea.

  2. United States—History—Civil War, 1861-1865 Biography.

  3. United States—History—Civil War, 1861-1865 Sources.   I. Title.

E468.L38 1999

973.7—dc21   99-13047

                                       CIP

ISBN: 0-609-60255-1

10 9 8 7 6 5 4 3 2

First Edition

The CIVIL WAR

Unstilled Voices

A three-dimensional
interactive book

Chuck Lawliss

Crown Publishers, Inc.
New York

The FANATIC

THE BOOK THAT ROCKED THE COUNTRY

Harriet Beecher Stowe had spent exactly one weekend in a slave state. But she wrote a book on slavery that rocked America to its foundation. *Uncle Tom's Cabin* was sentimental, patronizing, and implausible, but the depiction of the cruelty of slavery moved readers as nothing else had. Despite the book being banned in the South, more than 300,000 copies were sold in the United States within a year of its publication in 1852. No previous book in America had ever come close to selling so many copies so quickly. By 1861, a million-and-a-half copies were in print worldwide. Queen Victoria is said to have wept over the book. Harriet Beecher Stowe said that God inspired the book and that the climactic scene, the death of noble Uncle Tom, came to her in a vision while she sat in church. When President Lincoln met the author, he greeted her with the words: "So this is the little woman who wrote the book that made this great war."

135,000 SETS, 270,000 VOLUMES SOLD.

UNCLE TOM'S CABIN

FOR SALE HERE.

AN EDITION FOR THE MILLION, COMPLETE IN 1 Vol., PRICE 37 1-2 CENTS.

" " IN GERMAN, IN 1 Vol. PRICE 50 CENTS.

" " IN 2 Vols., CLOTH, 6 PLATES, PRICE $1.50.

SUPERB ILLUSTRATED EDITION, IN 1 Vol, WITH 153 ENGRAVINGS.

PRICES FROM $2.50 TO $5.00.

The Greatest Book of the Age.

JOHN BROWN BELIEVED he was the agent of God, personally chosen to free the slaves. He was a curious choice: an inept businessman who had failed twenty times in six states and who routinely defaulted on his debts, a poor father who regularly beat his twenty children for minor transgressions. He also was a cold-blooded killer. In the Kansas Territory, he and four of his sons hacked to death five slavery supporters. Brown said that he was simply defeating "Satan and his legions." Most people believed Brown was a dangerous lunatic and gave him a wide berth. Burly,

bearded, and wild-eyed, he resembled an Old Testament prophet. He quoted the Bible to support his beliefs and actions. "Without shedding of blood there is no remission of sin" was his favorite passage. Brown attracted the support of a small group of influential abolitionists. Among them were a minister, a college professor, and the noted black leader and former slave Frederick Douglass. Brown concocted a plan to free the slaves, and these men gave him the money to carry it out. He and a small band of followers would seize firearms stored in the arsenal at Harpers Ferry, (West) Virginia, arm the slaves, and ignite a black rebellion across the South. The October 1859 raid was, simply, a fiasco. Angry townspeople surrounded the engine house and began firing. Ironically, the first casualty was the baggage master at the railroad station—a free black—shot dead by Brown's men. Before it was over, ten of Brown's men were dead, including two of his sons. Brown was charged with murder, treason, and insurrection. He knew he would hang, but he wanted his death to count for something. He told the court: "Had I interfered in the manner which I admit…in behalf of the rich, the powerful, the intelligent, the so-called great, or in behalf of any of their friends, it would have been all right and every man in this Court would have deemed it an act worthy of reward rather than punishment." On the gallows, Brown handed a prophetic note to one of his guards: "I, John Brown, am now quite certain that the crimes of this guilty land will never be purged away but with

Blood…" 🔫 In the North, widespread admiration for Brown's courage was evidence of a deeply rooted anti-slavery sentiment. This stunned the South, which could not comprehend the extent of the sympathy for a fanatic bent on inciting a slave uprising. 🔫 The countdown to war had begun. In a little more than a year, Union troops would march off to war singing, "John Brown's body lies a-moldering in the grave, but his soul goes marching on…"

THE SUPREME COURT SUPPORTS SLAVERY

In 1857 the U.S. Supreme Court ruled in favor of slavery. The case involved Dred Scott, a Missouri slave. His owner, an army surgeon, had taken Scott with him to Illinois and Wisconsin, where slavery was illegal. Scott claimed the years he spent on free soil had made him a free man. The Court ruled that Scott had no right to sue. Blacks "…had no rights which a white man was bound to respect." A slave was his owner's property, and slaveholders could take their property anywhere they wished. This ruling had a widespread [implica]tion: It was now unconstitutional for [Congress to] pass legislation governing slavery. Southerners hailed the ruling as a victory. More and more Northerners began to agree with John Brown: slavery had no peaceful solution.

John Brown disappointed his supporters by saying nothing from the gallows, but they soon learned that on the way to his execution, Brown had handed a guard a short note.

The PRESIDENTS

ABRAHAM LINCOLN AND JEFFERSON DAVIS were fellow Kentuckians, born only eight months and a hundred miles apart. Both tall and thin, they were voracious readers and gifted public speakers. Each loved his country and became president on the eve of war. ⚓ In other respects, the two men were quite different. Davis, a graduate of West Point, was refined and cultured. Lincoln, a product of the Western frontier, was self-educated and unpolished. Davis was experienced in military and public affairs; Lincoln wasn't. Davis looked like an aristocrat; Lincoln looked like the rail-splitter he once was. ⚓ Davis should have been the better president. Yet most Americans consider Lincoln the greatest of all presidents. Davis is seen as ineffective and, in some respects, a failure. ⚓ An effective politician in Illinois in the mid–1850s, Lincoln could amuse people with his homespun stories and excite them with political speeches. After one uneventful term in the United States Congress, he joined the new Republican party and ran against Stephen A. Douglas for the U. S. Senate. Lincoln lost, but his success in his debates with Douglas brought him national recognition. ⚓ Elected president in 1860, Lincoln faced endless crises that would have shattered a weaker man. Criticism of him was constant and loud. He had to cope with jealous politicians and unsuccessful generals. As the war dragged on, military defeats and high numbers of casualties stunned the nation, and many doubted if the war could be won. Lincoln was courageous, tough when necessary, and determined to preserve the Union. Even during the nation's darkest hours, he displayed coolness and held his temper. ⚓ Lincoln loved the people. He spent hours talking with common folk. He visited army hospitals and greeted soldiers in the front lines. People thought of him as a father and called him "Old Abe." In 1863 when he called for 100,000 new troops, the response was so great that a new war song appeared: "We Are Coming, Father Abraham, Three Hundred Thousand Strong." ⚓ Lincoln possessed an extraordinary ability to see people as they were. He had no time for braggarts and fired those who did not perform well. But when he found capable people, he gave them the support they needed to do their job well. ⚓ To preserve the Union, Lincoln often violated the

Constitution by exceeding the powers of his office. He shut down antiwar newspapers and arrested people of questionable loyalties. At times he usurped powers that belonged to Congress, and he ignored Congress when he felt it was necessary. This frightened many people, but those same actions helped bring victory.  When Lincoln was elected, few people felt he had the ability to be a successful president. Yet he grew stronger each year. He developed the knack of acting at precisely the right moment. Abraham Lincoln, the homely man in the frock coat and stovepipe hat, became the embodiment of all the best qualities of America. Lincoln's counterpart, Jefferson Davis, resigned from the U.S. Senate and returned home when Mississippi seceded. While the Confederacy was being organized, a telegram arrived. Davis's wife recalled, "He looked so grieved that I feared some evil had befallen our family. After a few minutes, he told me [what it contained] as a man might speak of a sentence of death." Davis had been elected President of the Confederacy. As president, Davis proved to be his own worst enemy. Flaws in his character appeared early in the war and grew larger as the struggle grew more intense. He was a poor administrator, unaccustomed to giving direction to large numbers of people. He habitually chose the wrong men for jobs, appointing incompetents to government posts, and would not leave able assistants alone to do their work. Fascinated by details, he was a slow worker who failed to keep pace with the scores of problems that demanded his attention. Davis did not know how to gain favor with the people. He couldn't mingle easily in a crowd. He appeared aloof and distant. Even his longtime colleague Stephen Mallory admitted that "few men could be more chillingly, freezingly cold" than the Confederate president. Davis had a short temper and fought constantly with other Southern leaders. He quarreled with his vice president, congressmen, cabinet members, generals, and governors. He was impatient with those who disagreed with him. His own wife admitted that "he did not know the arts of a politician and would not practice them if understood." He gave too much time to military affairs and too little to social, economic, and political matters where he could have been useful. Ill health sapped his effectiveness. During most of his presidency, he suffered from a variety of ailments: indigestion, boils, a nervous disorder, insomnia, and migraine headaches. In his favor, however, it must be said that Jefferson Davis's loyalty was unquestioned, and he nearly worked himself to death for his beloved Confederacy. Like Abraham Lincoln, Jefferson Davis was willing to die for the cause and country he so desperately loved.

The DIARIST

MARY ON MEN

"All the comfort of my life depends upon his being in a good humor," Mary wrote of her husband. Southern society was dominated by men, and peace and harmony depended on masculine needs being promptly met. "James Chesnut has been so nice this winter," she wrote in her diary, "so reasonable and considerate—that is, for a man." Of her friend Nathan Davis, Mary Chesnut wrote: "Nathan, all the world knows, is by profession a handsome man." Another friend, Edmund Rhett, was famous for his "very fine eyes and makes fearful play with them." Mary's diary contains an unsentimental portrait of her father-in-law: "Partly patriarch, partly grand seigneur, this old man is of a species that we will see no more; the last of the lordly planters who ruled the Southern world... He came of a race that would brook no interference with their own sweet will by man, woman, or devil."

MARY CHESNUT WAS the epitome of South Carolina plantation aristocracy, as was her husband, James, a U.S. senator when their state seceded. During the war, the Chesnuts were close friends of the Jefferson Davises, and James was an advisor to the Confederate president. Despite all this, Mary's place in history would be merely a footnote if not for her diary. In an age when keeping a diary was a popular pastime, Mary's diary was exceptional. She wrote with wit and candor of everything that went on around her. Her diary reveals what life was like in the highest levels of the wartime Confederacy. Mary described herself as a "tolerably close observer, a faithful watcher… from my youth upward of men and manners." Her observations were as accurate and as deadly as a sniper's rifle. She sensed the Union was breaking up: "These foolish, rash, hare-brained Southern lads…are thrilling with fiery ardor. The red-hot Southern martial spirit is in the air." When secession came, she saw it through the eyes of a wife. "We are divorced, North from South, because we hated each other so." The Chesnuts were in Charleston on April 12, 1861, when a mortar shell arched above the harbor and exploded directly

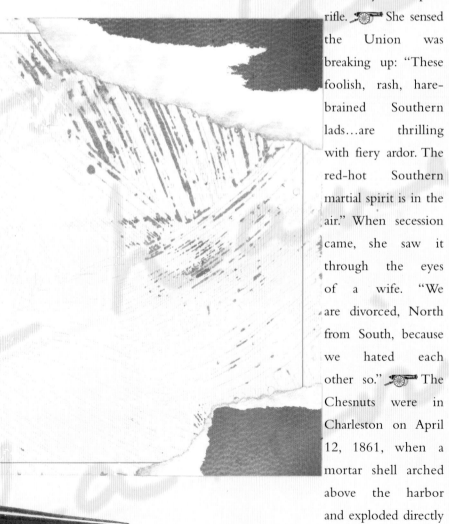

over Fort Sumter. Within minutes, forty-three guns opened fire, pounding the Union fort constantly for thirty-four hours. Two days later, the commander of the fort, Major Robert Anderson, agreed to surrender. The next day Lincoln called out 75,000 troops. The war had begun. Mary Chesnut chronicled the fateful days before the attack (her account of the attack appears in the diary excerpt at left): "Things are happening so fast," she wrote. "My husband has been made an aide-de-camp of General Beauregard…Now he tells me the attack upon Fort Sumter may begin tonight." In her April 12, 1861, entry, Mary wrote: "[It] was the merriest, maddest dinner we have had yet. Men were more audaciously wise and witty. We had an unspoken foreboding it was to be our last pleasant meeting." Later that night: "I do not pretend to go to sleep. How can I? If Anderson does not accept terms at four o'clock, the orders are he shall be fired upon…At half past four, the heavy booming of a cannon! I sprang out of bed and on my knees, prostrate, I prayed as I never prayed before." The bombardment was so heavy, Mary sought out other frightened souls. "I put on my double-gown and a shawl and went, too. It was to the housetop. The shells were bursting…And who could tell what each volley accomplished of death and destruction…The women were wild, there on the housetop. Prayers from the women and imprecations from the men, then a shell would light up the scene…" Mary Chesnut knew many leaders of the Confederacy, and believed their biggest flaw was their inability to work together. "We are abusing one another as fiercely as ever we abused Yankees," she wrote in 1861. Early in the war, Mary sensed how it would end: "Slavery has to go, of course," adding strikingly, "and joy go with it." As the war drew to a close, her mood grew increasingly dark. "Is anything worth it—this fearful sacrifice; this awful penalty we pay for war…The deep waters are closing over us…Darkest of all Decembers ever my life has known, sitting here by the embers, stunned, helpless, alone." Her words were as beautiful as her despair was deep. After the war, the Chesnuts returned to their plantation and found the house stripped by Union soldiers and the cotton burned. Mary managed to make a little money selling butter and eggs in partnership with her faithful maid. Childless, Mary Chesnut died in 1886, and left her diary to a friend.

MARY'S ENDURING LEGACY

As years passed, Mary's diary took on a life of its own. An abridged and censored version, titled *A Diary from Dixie,* was published in 1905. In 1981, nearly a century after her death, a restored and revised version of her diary was published. Titled *Mary Chesnut's Civil War,* it won a Pulitzer Prize.

Confederate forces attack Fort Sumter.

COMMANDERS

ULYSSES S. GRANT and Robert E. Lee were the greatest generals of the war. Beyond that, they had little in common. No one thought Grant would amount to anything. His father thought he was lazy with no business sense, and secured him an appointment to West Point. Grant arrived to find his name had been entered incorrectly—Ulysses S. Grant rather than Hiram Ulysses Grant. He accepted the new moniker. He didn't want to make a fuss. Lee, on the other hand, seemed destined for greatness. He was born on one of Virginia's great plantations to a Revolutionary War hero and the daughter of the wealthiest man in the state. But Robert's father made disastrous investments, lost the plantation, and went to debtors' prison. The family subsisted on the charity of relatives and Robert's mother became an invalid. Robert aspired to become a doctor, but lack of money led him to West Point instead. "Sam," as Grant was called by his friends, was shy and awkward. He accumulated demerits for oversleeping and slovenly dress. He excelled only at horsemanship. He graduated 21st among the 39 members of the class of 1843. Lee had a brilliant record at West Point, graduating in 1829. He was commander of the corps of cadets and second in his class scholastically, his record unblemished by a single demerit. Both Lee and Grant fought in the Mexican War. Major Lee served with distinction on the staff of Commander-in-Chief Winfield Scott, who called him "the best soldier I ever saw in the field." Lieutenant Grant was cited twice for heroism, once in a dispatch written by Lee. Later, stationed in the West, Grant began drinking heavily. He resigned from the army in 1854 rather than be court-martialed for drunkenness. Back home, Grant failed at a number of civilian jobs before going to work in his father's leather-goods store. While Grant was having his troubles, Lee was the commandant of West Point. Colonel Lee led the troops that captured John Brown at Harpers Ferry. The war saved Grant.

A dignified Robert E. Lee surrendered at Appomattox Court House.

He took command of an Illinois regiment and headed south into history. Grant said little and usually had a cigar in his mouth. A staff officer noted that Grant's usual expression was that of a man who had made up his mind to drive his head through a stone wall.  The war forced Lee to make a hard choice. He deeply loved the Union, but when he was offered supreme command of all Union armies, he resigned rather than raise his sword against his native state. When Virginia joined the Confederacy, Lee did the same. He took command of Virginia's forces in the first months of the war, and then served as military adviser to President Davis. The war was a year old before Lee was given command of the Army of Northern Virginia. For three years, Lee demonstrated the brilliance of a born military leader. He could attack savagely and was a master of defense. Even in the final months of the war, when Lee's army was ragged, ill-equipped, and malnourished, he delivered three times the number of casualties that his army suffered. But Lee was a Southern gentleman, kind and modest, courteous and religious; he referred to the enemy as "those people." The war turned his hair gray and then ruined his health. Grant's greatest quality was his determination. A Confederate general who knew him from West Point said: "That man will fight us every day and every hour until the end of the war." Grant did just that. Beginning with Fort Henry and Fort Donelson, he moved from victory to victory. Unlike Lee, Grant did not take brilliant gambles and make flashing strikes; rather, he possessed a wide vision of the war. He had balanced judgment, dogged courage, common sense, and good luck. When a senator criticized Grant, President Lincoln simply said, "I can't spare this man. He fights." Lee and Grant first met in battle in May 1864 at The Wilderness, an area of scrub pine and underbrush near Fredericksburg, Virginia. For nearly a year they fought savagely, before Grant finally trapped Lee and forced him to surrender. The surrender ceremony was held in a farmhouse at Appomattox Courthouse. Lee arrived first, wearing his dress uniform. Grant came in his usual private's blouse with his trousers tucked into muddy boots. They chatted about the Mexican War before getting down to business. Grant's terms were generous. Lee's soldiers would be sent home on parole. Those who owned horses could keep them for use in plowing their fields. Grant also agreed to issue food to the half-starved Southern troops. Lee accepted the terms with gratitude. They saluted each other and parted. Lee told his troops: "Men, we have fought the war together, and I have done the best I could for you. You will all be paroled and go to your homes…" Tears flooded his eyes. He tried to continue, but only managed to say, "Good-bye."

9

The SOLDIERS

A WAVE OF PATRIOTIC FERVOR swept the North after Lincoln's call for volunteers. Recruiting rallies were held in every city and town, and young men flocked to the colors. "So anxious was I for starting," said one volunteer, "that I felt like ten thousand pins were pricking me in every part of my body." Southerners greeted the war with the same enthusiasm. "As one looks at the resolute, quick, angry faces about him," observed William Howard Russell, a British war correspondent, "...one must feel the South will never yield to the North..." Everyone thought it would be a short and glorious war. *The New York Times* predicted it would be over in thirty days; the *Chicago Tribune* thought it might take three months. Each side underestimated the other. "Just throw three or four shells among those blue-bellied Yankees," said a North Carolinian, "and they'll scatter like sheep." The North also was cocky: It had more of everything needed to win a war. The youngest Civil War soldier was a nine-year-old lad from Mississippi; the oldest was an eighty-year-old great-grandfather from Iowa. One out of every four Union soldiers was Irish, Norwegian, German, French, or some other European nationality and had come to America in search of a better life. Farm boys, students, merchants, blacksmiths, and clerks were the backbone of the armies. In total, three million Americans wore the blue of the North or the gray of the South. The typical soldier was a farmer, unmarried, and about twenty-one years old. He had two to three years of formal education. His writing was crude, and he tended to spell words as he spoke them—"git" for "get," "thar" for "there," "yestiddy" for "yesterday," and so on. Soldiers wrote as they thought, and sentences often had little connection to one another. Joining the army was the first time most of the soldiers had been away from home, and they were soon deeply homesick. The only contact with loved ones was by mail, and there was more letter writing in the Civil War than at any other time in American history. A Connecticut private wrote his sweetheart: "The soldier looks upon a letter from home as a perfect God send—sent as it were, by some kind ministering Angel Spirit, to cheer his dark and weary hours." Soldiers wrote about anything and everything. John Shank, an Illinois soldier, began a letter home with this statement: "There

THE RECRUITING EFFORT

At first there were so many volunteers that neither North nor South could handle them all. Later, when soldiers wrote home about their casualties and living conditions, fewer answered the call to the colors. Posters (like the one above) were displayed and rallies were held to attract new recruits. Both sides paid cash rewards for volunteers, and finally resorted to conscription to fill their ranks.

is a fly on my pen. I just rights What ever Comes in my head." ☞ Recruits soon lost their enthusiasm when they felt the painful shock of camp life. Equipment and training were poor, and food, quarters, and medical attention were worse.

Many officers did not know much more than their troops. Most soldiers never fully accepted the blind obedience and strict devotion to duty of the professional soldier. But their courage and steadfast commitment in the face of bloody battle and severe suffering have led some historians to rank them as the greatest fighting men of all time. ☞ Life in an army tent was uncomfortable at best. Usually six men slept in tents designed for only four. A smaller, two-man tent was known as a "dog shanty" or "pup tent" because, as one soldier explained, "it would only comfortably accommodate a dog, and a small one at that." ☞ Most young soldiers were religious and their prayers were often informal. Before a battle, a rebel private reportedly offered this plea: "Lord, if you aint for us, don't be agin us. Just step aside and watch one of the worst fights you are ever going to see." ☞ If life in the field was unpleasant, battle was hell on earth. The defenders would line up in two rows. The men in the front row knelt, guns in position; the back row stood ready to shoot over their heads. Swirling around the attackers were officers on horseback with swords flashing. The noise was deafening—explosions of muskets and cannon, men yelling, horses snorting. The smoke was blinding; no one could see what was happening, and in the confusion many soldiers were killed by their own side. ☞ What the average soldier dreaded almost as much as death was cowardice—"showing the white feather" in the face of the enemy. A Connecticut recruit wrote to his parents: "I hope as I always have, that I may have the courage to do my duty well, not recklessly but with simple bravery and fidelity, so that if I fall you may have the consolation of knowing that I not only lose my life in a good cause but die like a man." ☞ Battle changed the tone of the letters. After Shiloh, one Ohio private wrote: "God grant that I may never again be the partaker of such scenes." An Alabama sergeant commented: "This night of horrors will haunt me to the grave."

THE SOLDIER'S DIET

Army food was based on hardtack biscuits, salt beef, and pork. The soldiers called pork "salt junk" and beef "salt horse." When available, dried peas and beans were part of the meal. Hardtack could break a tooth and needed to be fried in pork fat or soaked in water before eating. The main meal was served at midday. Breakfast and supper consisted of bread and coffee. Strong coffee was an indispensable consolation, and the average Union soldier drank four pints a day. Coffee was a rare treat for Confederates, who made do with substitutes brewed from chicory or peanuts.

The BLACKS

THE WAR DIDN'T START out as a crusade to abolish slavery and, ironically, it initially intensified racial prejudice in the North. Some people blamed blacks for starting the war, and anti-black riots erupted in many cities. Newspapers warned of millions of "semi-savages" intermingling with "the sons and daughters" of white families, and of free labor being "degraded" by the competition of these blacks, who "will have to be supported as paupers and criminals at the public expense." When a delegation of black leaders visited Lincoln, they were appalled when he urged them to consider emigration instead of emancipation. "This is our country as much as it is yours," one told the president, "and we will not leave it." "Teach the rebels and traitors that the price they are to pay for the attempt to abolish this government must be the abolition of slavery," thundered Frederick Douglass, the most influential black leader in the country. In 1862, when Horace Greeley of the *New York Tribune* urged Lincoln to make freeing the slaves a war aim, the president replied: "My paramount object in this struggle is to save the Union, and is not either to save or destroy slavery…" Lincoln was fearful that a premature move against slavery would drive the border states of Kentucky and Missouri out of the Union. By the summer of 1862, however, he believed he could make abolition a goal of the war. But he first wanted a Union victory. Five days after Lee's invasion of the North was turned back at the Battle of Antietam, Lincoln issued the Emancipation Proclamation, which declared that all slaves in states still in rebellion on January 1, 1863, "shall be then, henceforward and forever

DRUMMER JACKSON

The Emancipation Proclamation allowed former slaves to enlist in the new segregated units, collectively called the U.S. Colored Troops. One of the younger recruits was a boy, known only as "Jackson," who was fitted with a uniform and renamed "Drummer Jackson."

free." It now was a war to free the slaves. When war came, thousands of Northern blacks tried in vain to enlist, only to be turned away. After the Emancipation Proclamation, large numbers of blacks were recruited and served in segregated units known as the U. S. Colored Troops. At first, black soldiers performed only menial tasks, and they were paid less than white soldiers. Some were abused and humiliated by their white officers. The turning point came on July 18, 1863, when 600 men of the all-black 54th Massachusetts Regiment assaulted Confederate-held Fort Wagner in South Carolina. Nearly half of them were wounded or killed. When the color-bearer fell and the order to withdraw was given, Sergeant William Carney seized the colors and made it back to his lines despite bullet wounds in the head, chest, right arm, and leg. He became the first of twenty-nine blacks during the war to be awarded the Medal of Honor—although he had to wait thirty-seven years to receive it. "It is not too much to say that if this [black regiment] had faltered when its trial came," the *New York Tribune* editorialized, "200,000 troops for whom it was a pioneer would never have put into the field…But it did not falter. It made Fort Wagner such a name for the colored race as Bunker Hill had been for ninety years to the white Yankees." Abolitionist Wendell Phillips put it differently: "Will the slave fight? If any man asks you, tell him No. But if anyone asks you will a Negro fight, tell him Yes!" In the Confederate army, slaves were used as grooms, valets, teamsters, general laborers, and musicians. Half of the Confederate nurses were slaves. A few slaves supported the Confederate cause, but many more fled to Union lines as soon as the opportunity arose. In November 1864, President Davis and General Lee tried to enlist slaves as soldiers, offering them freedom after the war as an inducement to serve. Many politicians opposed the idea, and the war was nearly over before the proposal was enacted. The Georgia secessionist Howell Cobb summed it up: "If slaves will make good soldiers, our whole theory of slavery is wrong."

The Provost Guard of the 107th Colored Infantry.

A THIEF AND A ROBBER

The black conscience of the North was Frederick Douglass. Raised as a field hand and houseboy, he was taught to read and write by his master's wife. Determined to escape slavery, he succeeded on his second attempt. He was a laborer in Massachusetts in 1839 when he gave an impromptu speech at a meeting of the Anti-Slavery Society and found his destiny. A natural orator with a magnificent voice, he drew large crowds wherever he spoke. "I appear this evening as a thief and a robber," he would tell his audiences. "I stole this head, these limbs, this body from my master and ran off with them."

Fearing that he would be seized as a fugitive slave, Douglass sailed to England, lectured, and returned with enough money to purchase his freedom and found an abolitionist newspaper.

To Douglass the purpose of the war was clear. In 1861, he wrote in his newspaper, *Douglass' Monthly*: "Fire must be met with water, darkness with light, and war for the destruction of liberty must be met with war for the destruction of slavery."

The INVENTORS

FIGHTING ABOARD THE MONITOR

The men inside the Monitor and the Merrimack, half-blind with smoke, loaded and fired. "We went . . . as hard as we could," recalled a Union officer. "The shot, shell, grape, canister, musket, and rifle balls flew about in every direction, but did us no damage."

THE UNSUNG HEROES of the war were the inventors, and nowhere was their genius so apparent as in the war at sea. The Confederacy, which entered the war with no navy, converted a captured Union warship, the *Merrimack,* into a formidable ironclad battleship. On its first sortie, the *Merrimack,* renamed the *CSS Virginia,* destroyed two Union warships and ran a third aground. The Union had just built an ironclad of its own, a revolutionary design by John Ericsson, a brilliant Swedish immigrant. Lincoln likened it to "a cheesebox on a raft." Christened the *USS Monitor,* she had only two guns, but they were mounted in a revolving turret. The *Monitor* was launched in New York on January 30, 1862, and, by chance, was en route to Hampton Roads the day the *Merrimack* left her lair. Spectators crowded the shore when the ironclads met on March 9. As reported to Washington, they "fought, part of the time touching each other, from 8 a.m. to noon, when the *Merrimac* retired...The *Monitor* is uninjured and ready at any moment to repel another attack." Another inventor who aided the Union cause was James Buchanan Eads, a self-educated steamboat engineer from Saint Louis. He told Lincoln that a fleet of armor-plated steam-propelled gunboats was needed on the Mississippi. Lincoln agreed and the first boat was ready forty days later. His gunboats played a key role in the capture of Vicksburg. The Confederates built small torpedo boats called "Davids" to attack the Goliath-like Union warships blockading Southern ports. The first David rammed her torpedo into a Union ship off the coast of Charleston, causing expensive damage to the Northern ship but killing most of the David's crew. Then the Confederates tried a submarine, the *H. L. Hunley,* named after her inventor. It was 40 feet long, only 42 inches in diameter, and resembled a cigar. On the night of February 17, 1864, the submarine attacked the 1,264-ton *Housatonic* in Charleston Harbor. It rammed a canister of gunpowder into the frigate,

which lifted bodily out of the water before settling to the bottom, the first ship ever sunk by a submarine. Unfortunately, the submarine and its crew went down as well. To sell their creations, inventors crowded the waiting room at the War Department and buttonholed politicians. Most of them came away empty-handed, but a few saw their inventions change the way war was fought. During the war, the muzzle-loading musket replaced the flintlock, the breech-loading carbine replaced the muzzle-loaded musket, and the bullet replaced the musket ball. A musket was accurate to about fifty yards, but a sharpshooter with a rifle or a carbine could kill a man at 500 yards or more. The new weapons changed the dynamics of warfare: With muskets, the attackers had the advantage; with rifles, the defenders did. Curiously, breech-loading rifled artillery, used for the first time in the war, gave the advantage to the attacker. The guns, which fired shells rather than cannon balls, could be positioned beyond the range of the fort's cannons. Every brick and masonry fort in the world was made obsolete by rifled artillery. The machine gun, the cornerstone of modern infantry warfare, was invented by a Captain Williams of the Confederate Army, but it was flawed and saw little action. The first successful machine gun, which could fire hundreds of rounds a minute, was the Gatling gun. Invented by Dr. Richard Jordan Gatling, it was used by Union troops in the final months of the war. The Union War Department was always trying something new—tents, knapsacks, cooking utensils, saddles, and so on. When an Indianapolis grocer and former tinsmith came up with Van Camp's Pork and Beans, it soon was sustaining Union troops in the field. Military commanders adapted civilian inventions for their use. At Manassas, the first major battle of the war, the Confederates used Samuel F. B. Morse's new invention to order four brigades to come to their aid via the Manassas Gap Railroad—the first military use of the telegraph and the railroad in the United States. Celebrated balloonist Thaddeus Lowe organized a Balloon Corps for the Union army. Observers transmitted information to the ground using lightweight telegraph wire—the first aerial direction of artillery fire in history Ironically, one invention that could have shortened the war never saw action. Two inventors, B. Tyler Henry and Christopher Spencer, had perfected repeating rifles, but the Union War Department initially turned them down, reasoning that the weapons would encourage soldiers to waste ammunition.

THE TELEGRAPH'S ROLE

The transcontinental telegraph reached the Pacific Coast in 1861, just as the war was beginning. Both sides employed telegraphy extensively, used codes, and tapped the enemy's lines. Above, Thaddeus S.C. Lowe, in charge of observation balloons for the Union Army, telegraphs his findings to army headquarters.

The GENERALS

THE WAR PRODUCED more unforgettable generals than any other American struggle, before or since. Take William Tecumseh Sherman, for example. He seemed to be perpetually on the verge of a nervous breakdown. He talked rapidly in a high voice, often acted strangely, and his moods swung from rage to fright. Early in the war, General George McClellan gave the frenetic redhead an indefinite leave of absence. "Sherman's gone in the head," he explained. Ulysses S. Grant recalled him to duty, and later Sherman's March to the Sea proved to be the boldest, most effective stroke of the war. As a boy, Philip Sheridan wanted to go to West Point like his hero William Sherman. Phil was five-feet-five, weighed 115 pounds, and was a scrapper. He was suspended from West Point for a year for attacking a cadet who had insulted him. Sheridan later laid waste to the Shenandoah Valley. At Cedar Creek, "Little Phil" made his famous twenty-mile ride to turn the tide of battle for the Union. George Armstrong Custer graduated last in the West Point class of 1861, and three days later he was fighting at First Manassas. He went on to take part in virtually every battle fought by the Army of the Potomac. Headstrong and hungry for glory, Custer made many enemies, but he was idolized by millions for his courage and audacity. Fearless under fire, he had eleven horses shot from under him, yet was wounded only once. He was promoted to brigadier general at age twenty-three. The Confederacy had its share of eccentric leaders. Thomas Jackson, who earned the nickname "Stonewall" by his resolute stand at First Manassas, was fanatically religious and would not fight on Sunday unless attacked. He put together his own diet to fight dyspepsia (stomach troubles), and would not use pepper for fear it would make his left leg itch. He would ride for hours with his left arm above his head to stimulate his blood circulation. But battle exalted him. "I seem to have a more perfect command of my faculties in the midst of fighting," he explained. When Jackson was fatally shot by his own men, a grieving Lee said, "I do not know how to replace him." James Longstreet, who would become famous as Lee's "Old War Horse," was six-feet-two, powerfully built, with blue eyes and brown wavy hair. Voted the handsomest cadet while at West Point, he was a poor student and an indifferent soldier, preferring pranks to spit-and-polish. During the war, "Old Pete" rose quickly to the rank of lieutenant general. At Gettysburg, he did his best to dissuade Lee from making the attack known as "Pickett's Charge," and received much of the blame for its failure. The war's greatest cavalry leader was Nathan Bedford Forrest. The son of an illiterate blacksmith, he grew rich trading in land and slaves, and became a Confederate officer by equipping a cavalry battalion at his own

LETTER FROM THE FRONT

A field dispatch from Stonewall Jackson to Lee speaks volumes about his character. Jackson reveals his independence, aggressiveness, and religious belief. Also apparent is his loyalty; he once said he would follow Lee "into hell blindfolded."

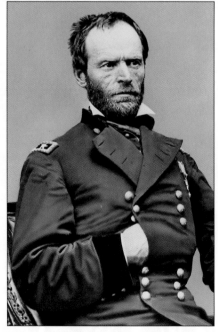

General William Tecumseh Sherman

expense. His daring raids on Union supply lines made him famous and led General Sherman to say Forrest had to be "hunted down and killed if it costs ten thousand lives and bankrupts the Federal Treasury." Forrest explained his military successes in simple terms. The winner, he said, is the one who "gits there furstest with the mostest." On the eve of war, the U.S. Army was pitifully small. It consisted of 1,108 officers and 15,269 enlisted men, most of whom were stationed in the West, protecting settlers from the Indians. A third of the officers resigned to join the Confederacy.

General James Longstreet

The large armies of the Civil War would require many generals, more than 1,000 by war's end. Only 300 of them, though, had served in the prewar army. Most of the new generals came from two areas. One was politics, the source of the "political generals," appointed because of their influence rather than military ability. Most proved to be costly misfits. The other group consisted of "civilian generals," men who entered the army at a lower rank and won their general's stars through superior performance. For many generals, it was a "brother officer's war." At First Manassas, P.G.T. Beauregard faced Irwin McDowell, both of the West Point class of 1838. Courted by two West Pointers, Ellen Marcy rejected A.P. Hill to marry George McClellan. Robert E. Lee's last graduating class while serving as West Point's commandant was 1855; twenty-three of that class served the Union, and fourteen the Confederacy. Most generals were young. A typical brigadier general was thirty-seven years old. The youngest was Galusha Pennypacker of Philadelphia, whose valor and five battle wounds made him a general by the age of twenty. The youngest Confederate general was John Kelly of Alabama: A general by the age of twenty-three, he was killed in battle ten months later. In the beginning, the South had the better generals. Most of the leading military schools of that day, such as the Virginia Military Institute and the Citadel, were in the South. Many of their graduates, along with Southerners who had attended West Point, had made the army a lifetime career. None of the important Union generals of 1861 was still in a command position by 1865. General after general tried unsuccessfully to lead the Army of the Potomac to victory, until Grant took command in 1864. A combination of Southern battle losses and the emergence of capable, hard-hitting Union commanders gave the advantage to the North late in the war.

LEE'S RIGHT ARM

At Chancellorsville, Lee sent Stonewall Jackson around the entire Union army to attack its right flank. Shortly after dark, the victorious Jackson was mortally wounded by shots from his own troops. Upon hearing the news, Lee said, "I have lost my right arm."

General Philip Sheridan

The SPIES

Belle Boyd

SOUTHERN WOMEN MADE good spies. Take Belle Boyd, for example. A vivacious, flirtatious young woman from Front Royal, Virginia, Belle was a born spy. While still in her teens, she used her girlish charms to coax military secrets out of Union officers, then rode through the night to give her information to Stonewall Jackson, who made her an honorary captain in his army. Before she was twenty-one, Belle had been reported to Union authorities thirty times, arrested seven times, and imprisoned twice. While in Washington's Old Capitol Prison, an unrepentant Belle continued passing on information by placing messages in hollow rubber balls and tossing them through the bars of her window to an accomplice below. In 1863 Belle sailed to England, carrying messages from President Davis. A Union officer followed her, wooed her, and married her. After the war, she took to the lecture circuit, giving embellished accounts of her wartime exploits. Audiences loved "La Belle Rebelle," as she was fondly called by the French. When the war came, Rose O'Neal Greenhow, a wealthy, Southern-born widow, decided to stay in Washington and spy for the Confederacy. Tall with piercing black eyes and a theatrical style, she was an influential hostess in the capital, and her elegant home on Sixteenth Street drew a stream of rich and powerful visitors. In July 1861, Rose learned that Union commander Irvin McDowell was planning to attack the Confederate forces at Manassas, Virginia. She even found out the strength of General McDowell's force and the route he would take to Manassas. She sent a coded message to Confederate general P. G. T. Beauregard, who made use of her intelligence in winning the first major battle of the war. Rumors of Rose's activities reached Federal agents. Her house was placed under round-the-clock surveillance, but with the help of friends who came to visit, she continued to collect and pass on information to the South. Discovered, she was locked up in the Old Capitol Prison, where she remained for more than a year. When she was released, she went to the Confederacy where she was welcomed as a heroine. President Davis sent her to Europe to enlist support and raise money for the Confederacy. On her way home, her ship ran aground in a storm off the coast of North

Carolina. Rose tried to reach shore but, weighted down with gold sewn into her clothing, she drowned.

Elizabeth Van Lew, the daughter of a wealthy Richmond merchant, was educated in Philadelphia, where she learned to hate slavery. When her father died, she freed all the family slaves. During the war, Elizabeth was a Union spy. She reported on conditions in the Confederate capital, and used her home as a hideout for prison escapees. The house had a large secret room, reachable only by a hidden stairway. She once hid 100 men there after they dug their way out of Libby Prison. She hired black servants to carry coded messages out of town and through rebel lines. She even managed to install one of her former slaves as a maid in the Confederate White House. Her spy went undetected throughout the rest of the war. After the war, Ulysses S. Grant rewarded Elizabeth Van Lew for her valuable services by appointing her postmaster of Richmond. But until her death in 1900, her friends never spoke to her again.

Elizabeth Van Lew

Rose O'Neal Greenhow with her daughter in the Old Capitol Prison.

The NURSES

FIELD TREATMENT

An army surgeon's kit contained the few tools needed to treat wounded soldiers—knives and saws of various sizes for amputations; forceps to keep a wound open and extract bits of shrapnel; catheters to draw off blood from the wound; various bandages and tourniquets; and anesthesia, if available.

"THEY'VE COME! THEY'VE COME!" The shouts awakened Louisa May Alcott and, by the time she was dressed, forty horse-drawn ambulances were awaiting outside the hospital door. A volunteer nurse in a Washington hospital, she would be attending wounded soldiers for the first time. She would recall: "The sight of several stretchers, each with its legless, armless, or desperately wounded occupant, entering my ward, admonished me that I was there to work, not to wonder or weep. So I corked up my feelings, and returned to the path of duty." More than 3,000 women served as army nurses, traditionally a male profession. Most of them were away from home for the first time. Some simply wanted to serve, while others wished to escape from a boring life. Few had any medical training or previous work experience. Suddenly these women were thrust into a frightening world of nauseating odors and haunting cries, where death was commonplace. Nurses cared for soldiers with pneumonia, dysentery, typhoid, and other diseases, with no vaccines to prevent the spread of infection. According to Louisa May Alcott, these nurses spent their

After the Battle of June 27th, the wounded were treated in the shade of a tree at a nearby field hospital.

time on duty "washing faces, serving rations, giving medicine, and sitting in a very hard chair." They were also surrogate mothers—reading to patients, helping them to write home, wiping their feverish faces, even singing lullabies to them. Field hospitals were particularly hard on women nurses, but most of them proved to be up to the task. From Gettysburg, nurse Cornelia Hancock wrote to her mother that even amputations

Clara Barton

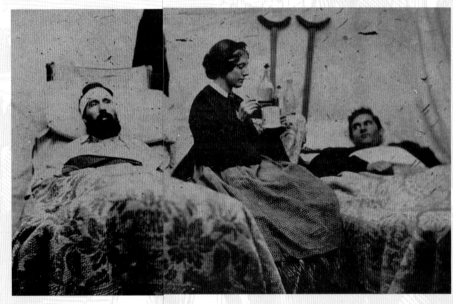

no longer bothered her. "Their screams of agony do not make as much impression on me now as the reading of this letter will on you," she wrote. At Shiloh, Confederate nurse Kate Cumming wrote in her diary: "The foul air from this mass of human beings at first made me giddy and sick, but I soon got over it. We have to walk…in blood and water, but we think nothing of it at all. In Richmond, Sally Tompkins established and subsidized a twenty-two-bed hospital in a friend's mansion, treating 1,333 wounded rebel soldiers during the war. Because of her excellent sanitary standards and quality of care, her hospital had the lowest death rate of any Confederate hospital. When all hospitals were put under army control, President Davis made her a captain to allow her to continue her work. Sally Tompkins was the only woman ever to hold a commission in the Confederate Army. Clara Barton, who nursed Union soldiers at several battlefields and would later found the American Red Cross, worked on her own. She loaded her wagon with medical supplies and food and set off, often arriving before the fighting was over. Called "the angel of the battlefield," Clara Barton used a pocketknife to dig out bullets and wrapped wounds with bandages or corn husks. Despite the horror and hard work, most of the nurses would remember the war as the most exciting time of their lives. Katharine Wormeley said she had lived an entire lifetime during her three months as a nurse on a Federal hospital ship. As she wrote to a friend—"This is Life!"

PAVING THE WAY

For the first time in American history, women in the North and South served as army nurses, and their task was made more difficult by the prejudice of doctors and male nurses. Soon they had won the respect of their superiors and the appreciation of their patients.

The PRISONERS

Wednesday, June 8: A very hot day…I cannot stand the hot sun have to stay in the shade it makes my head ache and dizzy. Drew very small ration did not get them til after dark.

Thursday, June 9: Showery, men are dying at the rate of 60 every 24 hours mostly of scurvy and diarhea thousands not even as blanket for cover. Water is poor and dirty, fighting occurs several times every day, alas for human depravity.

Friday, June 10: Every day is very hot this the first day this month that we have not had a shower. If our government lets us remain here through the summer I have little hope of ever seeing home again.

THESE ARE EXCERPTS from a diary kept by Private George Crosby of Brattleboro, Vermont, while imprisoned at Andersonville, the largest military prison camp in the South. Of the 401 Vermonters captured with Crosby in the Battle of the Wilderness in Virginia, more than half died within six months. Prisoners of war suffered appallingly. Some 194,743 Union soldiers were captured, and 30,218 died in prison camps; some 214,865 Confederates were captured, and 25,976 died in prison camps. At Andersonville, some 33,000 prisoners were crowded into a space designed to hold 10,000. Forbidden to build shelters, they lived in holes scratched in the ground, which were covered by a tattered blanket. The daily food ration was a teaspoon of salt, three tablespoons of beans, and a half-pint of cornmeal. Drinking water came from a small creek that ran through the camp, a creek that also served as a sewer. By war's end, 12,912 graves were dug at Andersonville. The actual number of prisoners that died there is unknown. At the outset of the war, both North and South had to find ways to care for thousands of prisoners. Initially, prisoners were paroled on the promise not to fight in the war again. When this practice broke down, whatever buildings were available served to house prisoners—army training camps, a former medical college,

A POW'S ACCOUNT

Despite prison censorship, some inmates, such as the author of this letter, were able to correspond with family members and even send small tokens such as prison-made jewelry.

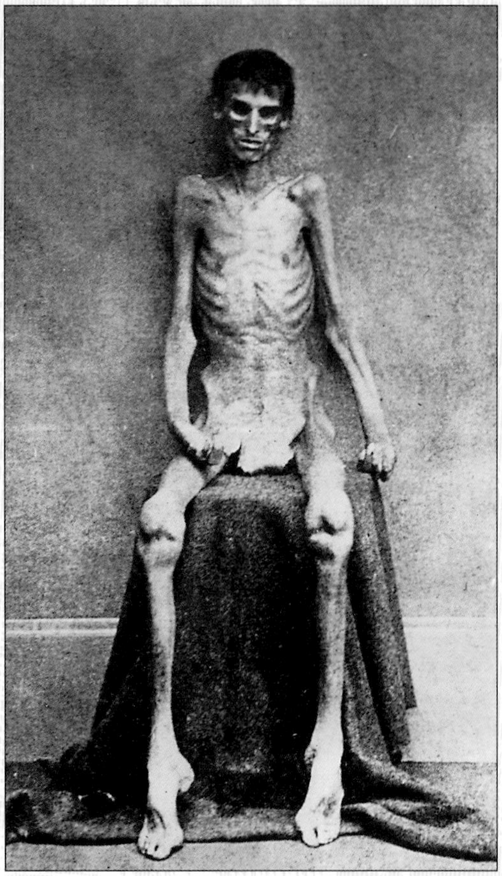

PHOTOGRAPHS OF ANDERSONVILLE

Prisoners, like the one shown at right, infuriated the North. People believed soldiers had been deliberately starved and mistreated. Public opinion demanded that these Confederate atrocities be avenged.

old forts, tobacco warehouses, slave pens. More than a year was spent working out a prisoner exchange system, but it eventually collapsed over the problem of exchanging black troops who were captured while serving in the Union army. To relieve the situation, the Confederacy built a number of prison camps in the Deep South, including Andersonville. The most common problem confronting prisoners in both the North and South was disease, bred by overcrowding, poor sanitation, and improper diet. The confined prisoners suffered terribly. Mismanagement brought on additional hardship. Andersonville commandant Hartman Heinrich Wirz, a Swiss immigrant, had enlisted in the Confederate army and lost the use of his right arm from a battle injury. Promoted to captain, he was sent to Andersonville. In the North, Wirz was considered to be the "monster...the fiend" responsible. Arrested at war's end, Wirz was brought to Washington and charged with war crimes. Found guilty, he was sentenced to hang. Shortly before his execution, Wirz was reputedly offered a reprieve in exchange for a statement that would convict Jefferson Davis of "conspiracy to murder prisoners." Wirz is said to have answered, "Jefferson Davis had no connection as to what was done at Andersonville. I know what orders are—I am being hung for obeying them." Henry Wirz became the only Confederate soldier to be executed for his actions during the war.

LIFE IN ANDERSONVILLE

Holding three times as many prisoners as originally intended, with almost no shelter, no sanitation, and only one source of water, it was not surprising that Andersonville meant death for thousands.

CIRCUMVENTING THE CENSOR

Prisoner mail was censored and sometimes not delivered or sent out. This Confederate soldier's pleasant depiction of the infamous Rock Island Prison satisfied the prison guards who were acting as censors.

23

The PHOTOGRAPHERS

"WE RECOGNIZED THE BATTLEFIELD as a reality, but it stands as a remote one....Like a funeral next door...Mr. Brady has done something to bring home to us the terrible reality and earnestness of war," said *The New York Times.* "If he has not brought bodies and laid them in our dooryards and along streets, he has done something very like it." The newspaper was reviewing an exhibit at Mathew Brady's New York City gallery of photographs taken within hours after the battle of Antietam, Maryland, in October 1862. The photographs on display ended once and for all the public's romantic notions of the war. The exhibit, The Dead at Antietam, shocked viewers. Photography was still a novelty in the 1860s, used primarily for making studio portraits. No one anything remotely like these photographs of the corpses of young men, lying with their arms

THE CAMERA

This vintage camera is compact compared to most cameras used in the war. It is mounted on a wooden stand instead of a bulky tripod, and uses film smaller than the conventional 8 x 10-inch or 11 x 14-inch sizes.

BRINGING THE HORROR HOME

The Civil War was the first to be extensively recorded on film, and it was a shocking experience to see photographs like this of dead soldiers lying on the battlefield, the work of Mathew Brady and his staff. After the war, books of war photographs were best-sellers.

outstretched, their lifeless bodies swollen and twisted. ⚙️ Brady was the most famous photographer of his time, and the most ambitious. He was born in upstate New York, the youngest of five children. He had a knack of attracting mentors. A painter named William Page taught him composition and portraiture. Then he met Samuel F. B. Morse, the inventor of the telegraph and an accomplished painter, who taught Brady the fundamentals of photography. ⚙️ Brady was a good student. By the age of nineteen, he had a studio in New York and was soon photographing the celebrated figures of the day—presidents, actors, writers, military leaders. A book of his photographs became a best-seller. He opened another studio in Washington, and among his subjects was the new president, Abraham Lincoln. When war came, Brady went to Lincoln and convinced the new president to authorize him to accompany the Union army and photograph the war at his own expense. "I felt I had to go," he recalled. "A spirit in my feet said go and I went." ⚙️ Brady photographed Manassas—where the first major battle of the war was fought—and nearly lost his wagon of bulky equipment in the confusion. The war soon grew too big for him to cover by himself. He hired outstanding photographers, organized them into teams, and sent them into the field. Brady's team at Antietam consisted of James Gibson and Alexander Gardner. Gardner, who had managed Brady's studio, was furious when all the Antietam photographs were labeled "Photo by Brady." Soon after, he left Brady and became the official photographer for General George B. McClellan, commander of the Army of the Potomac. Gardner later hired two of Brady's best photographers—Timothy O'Sullivan and Guy Fowx—and opened his own studio in Washington. ⚙️ Although Brady is remembered as the photographer of the Civil War, the war was his undoing. The huge amounts of money he spent to photograph the war plunged him into debt. Although he managed to sell 5,712 wartime negatives to the government for $25,000, he spent his final years in near poverty. He died in 1896 in a charity hospital. ⚙️ His ambitious goal had been to record all of the "prominent incidents of the conflict," and he succeeded. Other photographers in his time were more creative, but he was the first to understand the significance of photography. It was Brady who first realized that photography was visual history and could serve the nation's memory. ⚙️ Carl Sandburg wrote that Brady proved what photography could do by telling what "neither the tongues nor the letters of soldiers could tell of troops in camp, on the march, or mute and bullet-ridden on the ground." ⚙️ Brady, said Sandburg, "served history and country."

WARTIME PHOTOGRAPHY WAS NO SNAP

The photographic process was slow and the equipment bulky. Mathew Brady and his teams used horse-drawn wagons to carry equipment and serve as portable darkrooms. Cameras, which could weigh as much as twenty-five pounds, were too cumbersome to be held by hand. A tripod or other support was needed to steady the camera for the exposure, fifteen seconds or more. The plate upon which the image was to be recorded was prepared in advance. A sheet of copper, coated with silver and buffed, was washed in a solution of nitric acid to make it perfectly clean. Then it was treated with iodine vapor, which made it sensitive to light.

When everything was ready, the plate was inserted into the camera. The photographer removed the lens cap and hoped that nothing moved during the exposure to blur the photograph. The plate then was removed and developed. Even with no distractions, it took some thirty minutes to take a single photograph.

The FOLKS AT HOME

THE UNION FUND-RAISER

The war was costing the Union $2 million a day. The man responsible for raising that money was

Salmon P. Chase, an ambitious lawyer and abolitionist who, until Lincoln came along, was the star of the Republican Party. Although Chase had no financial background, Lincoln appointed him Secretary of the Treasury, apparently to neutralize a rival.

The president, though, came to value Chase and his political savvy. In 1862, when the Treasury was nearly broke, Lincoln lamented, "...the bottom is out of the tub. What shall I do?" Chase knew what to do. He worked diligently to get Congress to pass two acts that revolutionized the government's fund-raising methods. The first allowed the U.S. Treasury to issue paper money to replace gold as legal tender. The other was the income tax. The Internal Revenue Act of 1862 taxed virtually everyone and everything.

Political ambition got the better of Chase. He opposed Lincoln's reconstruction aims, and he secretly agreed to make a bid for the Republican nomination in 1864. When this leaked out, Chase offered Lincoln his resignation, but Lincoln refused to accept it. Chase campaigned for Lincoln, but when he again offered to resign, Lincoln let him go. He continued to value Chase's abilities, and a few months later appointed him chief justice of the Supreme Court.

"THE ROMANCE OF the thing is entirely worn off," Private J. H. Langhorne, with the Stonewall Jackson brigade, wrote to his mother, "not only with myself but with the whole army." It was the winter of 1861–1862, and the realities of war were becoming painfully apparent to the North and South, soldiers and civilians alike. The change was reflected in popular music. At first people sang "Battle Hymn of the Republic" and "Dixie"; now the songs were sadder, more thoughtful—"Just Before the Battle, Mother," "Tenting on the Old Camp Ground," and "When This Cruel War Is Over." More and more soldiers were needed, and both sides introduced conscription—and ways to avoid it. A Southern who owned twenty or more slaves was exempt from the draft. Northern draftees could hire substitutes. On both sides of the Mason-Dixon Line, people complained that it was "a rich man's war, but a poor man's fight." The North seemed little affected by the war. Its population continued to grow. Jobs were plentiful. No one was going hungry. New states were admitted (Kansas, Nevada). New colleges were founded (Vassar, University of Colorado). Railroads were built in the West, and settlers received free land under the new Homestead Act. John Wanamaker and Marshall Field opened stores. Central Park was created in New York City (see image at right). In Washington, the dome on the Capitol was completed. Other diversions during the war years included a new racetrack at Saratoga Springs, New York, and the midget General Tom Thumb at P. T. Barnum's Museum in New York City. Children played leap-frog and Simon Says, while their elders danced the waltz and the two-step. The income tax was introduced, taking 3 percent from the fortunate few who earned more than $800 a year. Meanwhile, the South was falling apart. It had less of everything. On the eve of war, there were more than twenty-two million people in the North; the South had nine million, more than a third of them slaves.

TRANSCRIPTIONS

The Diarist (page 6)

32

1861

April 12—

Anderson will not capitulate.

———————————

Yesterday was the merriest, maddest dinner we have had yet. Men were audaciously wise and witty. We had an unspoken fore boding it was to be our last pleasant meeting. Mr. Miles dined with us to day. Mrs. Henry King rushed in. "The news, I come for the latest news—all of the men of the King family are on the island."—of which fact she seemed proud.

While she was here our peace negotiator—or envoy—came in. That is, Mr. Chesnut returned. His interview with Col Anderson had been deeply interesting—but Mr. Chesnut was not inclined to be communicative. He wanted his dinner. He felt for Anderson and had telegraphed to President Davis for instructions.

What answer to give Anderson—&c&c.

33

He has now gone back to Fort Sumter, with additional instructions—

When they were about to leave the wharf—A H Boykin sprang into the boat in great excitement; he though himself ill used with a likelihood of fighting—and he to be left behind!

———————————

I do not pretend to go to sleep. How can I? If Anderson does not accept terms—at four—the orders are—he shall be fired upon—

I count four by St Michel chimes. I begin to hope. At half past four—the heavy booming of a cannon.

I sprang out of bed. And on my knees—prostrate—I prayed as I never prayed before.

There was a sound of stir all over the house. Pattering of feet in the corridor. All seemed hurrying one way. I put on my double

34

gown and a shawl and went too. It was to the house top.

The shells were bursting. In the dark I heard a man say "waste of ammunition."

I knew my husband was rowing about in a Boat somewhere in that dark bay. And that the shells were roofing it over—bursting Toward the Fort. If Anderson was obstinate—he was to order the Forts on our side to open fire. Certainly fire had begun. The regular roar of the cannon—there it was. And who could tell what each volley accomplished of death and destruction—

The women were wild, there on the house top. Prayers come from the women—and imprecations from the men. And then a shell would light up the scene. To night they say the forces are to attempt to land.

35

———————————

We watched up there and every body wondered. Fort Sumter did not fire a shot.

———————————

To day Miles and Manning—Cols. now—aides to Beauregard dined with us. The latter hoped I would keep the peace. I gave him only good words for he was to be under fire all day and night, in the bay carrying orders &c.

Last night—or this morning truly—up on the house top—I was so weary I sat down on something that looked like a black stool.

"Get up you foolish woman—your dress is on fire" cried a man. And he put me out. I was on a chimney, and the sparks had caught my clothes.

Susan Preston and Mr. Venable then came up. But my fire had been

36

extinguished before I broke out into a regular blaze.

———————————

Do you know, after all that noise and our tears and prayers—no body has been hurt, sound and fury signifying nothing, a delusion and a snare.

Louisa Hamilton comes here now. This is a sort of news center. Jack Hamilton—her handsome young husband has all the credit of a famous battery which is made of RR iron—Mr. Petigru calls it the Boomerang because it throws the balls back he way they came—so Lew H tells us. Hence the value of this lately achieved baby. She had no children during her first marriage. To divert Louisa from the glories of "the Battery" of which she raves, we asked if the baby could talk yet—

"—No—not exactly—but he imitates the big gun—when he hears that

37

he claps his hands and cries "Boom boom—" Her mind is distinctly occupied by three things—Leut Hamilton whom she calls "Randolph"— the baby—and the big gun—and it refuses to hold more.

Pryor of Virginia spoke from the Piazza of the Charleston Hotel.

I asked what he said—Irreverent woman—"oh they all say the same thing—but he made great play with that long hair of his, which he is always tossing aside."

———————————

Somebody came in just now and reported Col Chesnut asleep on the sofa in General Beauregard's room. After two such nights he must be so tired as to be able to sleep any where.

———————————

Just bade farewell to Langdon Cherev. He is forced to go home,

38

to leave this interesting place. Says he feels like the man who was not killed at Thermopolae. I think he said that unfortunate had to hang himself when he got home for very shame. May be fell on his sword which was a strictly classic way of ending matters.

———————————

I do not wonder at Louisa Hamilton's baby. We hear nothing, can listen to nothing. Boom Boom—goes the cannon—all the time—he nervous strain in awful, alone in this darkened room.

"Richmond and Washington, ablaze" say the papers. Blazing with excitement. Why not? To us these last days events seem frightfully great.

39

We were all women in that Iron Balcony—men we only see at a distance now. Start Means marching under the Piazza at the head of his regiment held his cap in his hand all the time he was in sight.

Mrs. Means was leaning over and when an unknown creature looking with tearful eyes asked "why did he take his hat off?" Mrs. Means stood straight up and said "he did that in honor of his mother. He saw me." She is a proud mother, and at the same time most unhappy. Her lovely daughter Emma is dying—in there—be fore her eyes—of consumption. At that I am sure Mrs. Means had a spasm of the heart. At least she looked as I feel sometimes. She took my arm—and we came in.

The Commanders (page 8)

?, Army in the Field
Camp near Donelson, Feb. 16th 1862

Gen. S. B. Buckner,
Confed. Army,

Sir, Yours of this date proposing armistice, and appointment of Commisioners, to settle terms of capitulation is just received. No terms except an unconditional and immediate surrender can be accepted.

I propose to move immediately upon your works. I am sir, very respectfully

Your obt. svt..
U.S. Grant
Brig. Gen.

The Generals (page 16)

Near 3 p.m.
May 2d, 1863

General,

The enemy has made a stand at Chancellor's which is about 2 miles from Chancellorsville. I hope as soon as practicable to attack.

I trust that an ever kind providence will help us with great success.

Respectfully,
T.J. Jackson
W. Genl.

Genl. R. E. Lee

The leading division is up and the next two appear to be well closed.

T.J.J.

The Spies (page 19)

Coded message reads:
LEE ATTACKS AT DAWN

The Prisoners (page 22)

Military Prison Rock
Island Illinois Aug. 31/64

My Dear Cousin

I received your kind letter acknowledging the receipt of the pin I was very glad to hear that you prise it so highly. You say you do not know how you will prove your appreciation that you have alredy done a dozen times. I wrote to cousin Lucy and directed, to Georgetown Ky not knowing that she was with you Tell her that I am a thousand times obliged to her for the tobacco which she was so kind to send me. I will in return send her a ring. You spoke of another cousin, having sent me some paper which I received and am under many obligations to her. Give me her name and I will send her a present of some kind. Enclosed you will find a "butter knife" of Rebel manufacture. If you will send me some silver and buttons. I will have you some nice rings made. Tell cousin Lucy Duke I would like very much to receive a letter from her and will take great pleasure in corresponding with her if she has no aversion to corresponding with a prisoner of war. I send you the picture of our row of Barracks with a limited portion of the balance of the prison. Give my kindest regards to my cousins of whom you speak.

Your affectionate cousin

Jas W. Duke
TAC43167

The Folks at Home (page 27)

Letter 1
1862
Summersville
May the 10
Dear and affectionnat

i now seat my self to in form you that i am well and hope thes few lines may find you in good helth and children all well. I'm good hart that this ware will soon come to a close and i will get to come home and our country will be restored to pease wonce more. i have just came in. i have binn out on a scout. we have binn out five days. we were after some horse theifs and Booshwhackers. thare was a bout too hundrend of them. our trupes are out after them yet and tha think thay will get them. we hung to of them the 9 of this month at sutton a bout thirty miles from summersvill. tha had killed a union boy a bout fiften years oald and the mail curry that carred the mail cross poul mountain. tha cut the boy open and stuck his head in sid. i think hanging was to good fore them. i recived your welcom letter and was glad to here that you and children was well and doing well. i hope that you and children will still will remain so and take care of your money that I send home to you. i want you to right as soon soon as this letter comes to hand and let me now what you are all doing. tell Sarry that i am well and hope thes few lines will find Sarry in good helth and in good hart. this is all at present time.

Isack Overall
Miss J. Overall

When thes few lines you read think that tha are from a husband that is fare from you and my dear children. Your affectionnat husban

I H Overall

Letter 2
July the 30th 1862 camp
meadow bluffs greenbier county Va

Dear Wife

I seat my self to inform you that i am well and i hope when thease few lines comes to hand that they may find you enjoying the same blessing.

i have not got much to write this time for i have not heard nothing of our men for so long that i cant say good bad nor indiferant about any thing more than we are all well and in good spirits. we have the best luck in our regiment of any in the bregade. However we had a litle bad luck last week in Summerville. the was two compnys of the 9th Verginnia thare to hold the poast and the rebles came in thare and captured the most of they men and the Liuetenant Colonel and a number of their rifles and 10,000 round of catrages but that was not the fault of the 36th at all for i am confident if we had a been theare that they could not taken neather amunition nor guns. we have no good news for so long that we would hardly know what good news was. i hope that we may hear something before long eather one way or the other and i do not care much witch you folks at home have a better chance than we have for we are shut up in camp so that we can not heare any thing only as we hear it from you folks at home as you send it in letters we have not yet been payed off but we expect to be before long. being as i have not get much to write i will send you enough paper to answer this one that i send.

I send my best respects to thee famley that moved in to Chambers burgh latley. i want you to write and lett me know how that was about ploughing the garden and how mutch he charged for it.

So nothing more at persant but remain your faithful Husband untill death.

Isaac Overall to Jane Overall

Write soon and give me the news in general.

Issac Overall

Letter 3
Murfreesboro Tenn
June 15th 1863

Dear aunt

With regret I seat my self to anounce the Death of Isaac. he Died the 5th of this month. he was taken sick near the first of may. he had the sore throat. he got nearly over that & then he rote to you that he was geting beter. he was then he tuck the pneumania. he tuck it be fore we left carthuye. he Didnt sufer vary much while we stayed thar. he was left thar in the huspitial. I dont no what hour he Died. Davvid kent rote to captin Henry stating that he Died the 5th. I Dont no how he Died, whuther he died eusey or not. I have told you all I no of his Death.

if they ar any thing you want to no, write to me & will find if I dont no. I am well my self at this tim

No mor but Remain yours
H I Nibert

ART AND PHOTO CREDITS

Leather and paper texture by Fred Thomas

The Fanatic (pages 2–3)
John Brown's capture (background): North Wind Picture Archives; *Uncle Tom's Cabin* poster: Corbis-Bettmann; Portrait of John Brown: Culver Pictures; *The Last Moments of John Brown*: Corbis-Bettmann; John Brown's note: Chicago Historical Society; Portrait of Dred Scott: Corbis-Bettmann

The Presidents (pages 4–5)
State Capitol at Montgomery (background): Corbis-Bettmann; Portrait of Abraham Lincoln: Corbis-Bettmann; Lincoln Political Cartoon: Boston Museum of Fine Arts; Lincoln's hat: Corbis-Bettmann; Portrait of Jefferson Davis: Culver Pictures; Davis Political Cartoon: Library of Congress.

The Diarist (pages 6–7)
Diary pages (background & inset): South Carolinian Library, University of South Carolina; Portrait of Mary Chesnut: South Carolinian Library, University of South Carolina; Pen & inkwell: Corbis-Bettmann; Bombardment of Fort Sumter: Corbis-Bettmann

The Commanders (pages 8–9)
Battle of Shiloh (background): Culver Pictures; Portrait of Ulysses S. Grant: Corbis-Bettmann; Grant's note: North Wind Picture Archives; Grant & Lee at Appomattox: Culver Pictures; Portrait of Robert E. Lee: Corbis-Bettmann; *The New York Times*: Timothy Hughes Rare & Early Newspapers; Map: Illustration by Matt Hutnak

The Soldiers (pages 10–11)
Second Bull Run (background): Corbis-Bettmann; Union Army draft poster: Corbis-Bettmann; Tin cup: Museum of the Confederacy; Union Army encampment: Corbis-Bettmann; Winter at Petersburg, Vermont: Corbis-Bettmann

The Blacks (pages 12–13)
Charge of the 54th Massachusetts colored regiment (background): Corbis-Bettmann; Contraband Jackson & Drummer Jackson: US Army Military History Institute; Company E, Fourth Colored Infantry: Corbis-Bettmann; Portrait of Frederick Douglass: National Archives; Men of Color recruiting poster: The Library Company of Philadelphia

The Inventors (pages 14–15)
Remington's Breech-loading fire-arm (background): Corbis-Bettmann; Monitor exterior: Corbis-Bettmann; Monitor interior: North Wind Picture Archives; Soldiers on deck of Monitor: Corbis-Bettmann; Thaddeus Lowe preparing telegraph message: Corbis-Bettmann

The Generals (pages 16–17)
Sheridan's Ride (background): Culver Pictures; Stonewall Jackson's note: North Wind Picture Archives; Portrait of William Tecumseh Sherman: Corbis-Bettmann; Portrait of James Longstreet: Corbis-Bettmann; Jackson being wounded by own men: North Wind Picture Archives; Portrait of Philip Sheridan: Corbis-Bettmann

The Spies (pages 18–19)
Receiving religious tracts from Belle Boyd (background): Culver Pictures; Portrait of Belle Boyd: Culver Pictures; Lacy fan: Corbis-Bettmann; Portrait of Elizabeth Van Lew: Cook Collection/The Valentine Museum; Rose O'Neal Greenhow with daughter in the courtyard of the Old Capitol Prison: Corbis-Bettmann; Confederate Secret Service coding disc: Museum of theConfederacy/Photo-graphy by Katherine Wetzel

The Nurses (pages 20–21)
Nurses taking care of wounded (background): Corbis-Bettmann; Surgeon's kits of Dr. Leonard Slater & Dr. Robert G. Rothrock: The Museum of the Confederacy/Photography by Katherine Wetzel; Field hospital after the Battle of June 27th: Corbis-Bettmann; Portrait of Clara Barton: Culver Pictures; Nurse with two patients: US Army Military History Institute; *Making Cartridges:* North Wind Picture Archives

The Prisoners (pages 22–23)
Prisoners at Andersonville (background): North Wind Picture Archives; Letter from James W. Duke to an unidentified cousin: Charles Buford Papers, Library of Congress; Union soldier after release from Andersonville: Corbis-Bettmann; Prisoner's sketch: Library of Congress; Rations being issued to prisoners at Andersonville: Corbis-Bettmann

The Photographers (pages 24–25)
Mathew Brady's photographic gallery at the Corner of Broadway and 10th Street (background): Corbis-Bettmann; Skaife's patent miniature brass camera, 1859: Corbis-Bettmann; Engineer Company, 8th New York State Militia: Culver Pictures; Four photographs in envelope—Dead Confederate (close up): Library of Congress, Confederate Dead at Antietam: National Archives, Dead Confederate: Library of Congress, Cleaning up after the battle of Cold Harbor: National Archives; Alexander Gardner standing near horse-drawn photographic supply wagon: Corbis-Bettmann

The Folks at Home (pages 26–27)
The terrace at Central Park (background & inset): Corbis-Bettmann; Portrait of Salmon P. Chase: Corbis-Bettmann; Confederate money: The Confederate Treasury Company; Letters to Jane Overall: Bernard C. Overall Jr. Family Letter Collection/Photography by Mary Rezny

The Assassin (pages 28–29)
Stage and proscenium boxes of Ford's Theater as they appeared on the night of President Lincoln's assassination (background): Culver Pictures; Reward poster: Culver Pictures; Portrait of John Wilkes Booth: Corbis-Bettmann; *Souvenir of the Assassination of President Lincoln by John Wilkes Booth at Ford's Theater (Scene of the Recent Deplorable Disaster)*: Corbis-Bettmann; "Our American Cousin" tickets: National Park Service/Ford's Theater National Historical Society; Execution of Lincoln conspirators: Culver Pictures